Apartamento Cookbook #7: Late-Night Meals

Apartamento Cookbook #7: Late-Night Meals

Drawings by Benoît François

apartamento

ANDONI LUIS ADURIZ
Sincronizada Sandwich with Blue Cheese and Anchovies

In my life I've been lucky enough to travel to several Latin American countries, and I've always been drawn to the latent traces of the history that Basque culture and Latin American culture share. For this recipe, I've found inspiration precisely in this Basque-Latin heritage. Migrations, from both sides, from yesterday and today, have left a permanent footprint on our identity. It's a story of exchange that began hundreds of years ago and reached its peak in the 19th century. This recipe is a tribute to that union, to that shared imagery: the centuries of history that unite the Basque and the Latin American, a confluence of products from here and from there. It's a quick and flavourful bite to be devoured after a long and intense day.

INGREDIENTS
Salted anchovies

For the corn tortillas
100g nixtamalized corn flour
10g cooked millet
1½g salt
20g Maseca
Water
(Or use shop-bought tortillas)

For the blue cheese and cider cream
50g quality blue cheese
25g natural cider

Serves 1

METHOD
To make the tortillas, blend all the ingredients together, adding water as needed until the dough is smooth. Make small balls of dough on parchment paper and flatten them with the help of more parchment paper and a smooth surface. For the cream, blend the blue cheese and cider together and set aside. Place a tortilla in a non-stick skillet over medium heat. Put a spoonful of the cream and 3 anchovies on the tortilla, then place another tortilla on top. Leave to cook for 3 minutes on each side, until the cheese has melted. Eat while hot!

PALISA ANDERSON
Mackerel Salad

I absolutely adore mackerel in any form. Give me blue oily fish before bed to quell hunger and put me to sleep belching spicy burps over dry turkey any day. Did you know blue oily fish has a good dose of tryptophan? The amino acid that helps make melatonin and serotonin, the hormones that send you off and keep you in good deep zzzs. If you've been out partying, this is a dish to throw together when you come home. It helps you wind down and is light enough to eat before bed to absorb all your sins. I have wonderful memories of my mum making a version of this for both late-night suppers after work or late breakfasts with simple rice congee, usually alongside multiple grazing dishes of pickled mustard and whatever happened to be in the fridge as leftovers. There's always a can of fish somewhere at the back of everyone's pantry, usually bought in a spurt of supermarket inspo. I'm hoping you will be growing the herbs in a pot somewhere to throw into the dish. The other ingredients are pretty standard in most people's kitchen these days, and if you don't have something, think like a migrant and substitute. Migrants are genius at subbing and adapting ingredients. That's how some of the most delicious ingenious dishes come into being. A moment of late-night inspired creativity can turn into something with long-lasting tingles for palates everywhere.

INGREDIENTS

200g can mackerel in tomato sauce
2 limes
1½ tbsp fish sauce
1 tsp coconut nectar
2 fresh bird's eye chilli, finely sliced
½ tsp prik pong (ground toasted bird's eye chilli)
2 garlic cloves, finely sliced
2 red shallots, thinly sliced
4 spring onions, thinly sliced
4 stems coriander, coarsely chopped
4 stems dill, coarsely chopped
A handful crisp fried shallots to garnish

Serves 2–3

METHOD

Drain the tomato sauce out of the can into a mixing bowl and whisk to combine with fish sauce, fresh and dried chilli, coconut nectar, and the zest and juice of the limes. Carefully place the mackerel back in and add the garlic, shallots, spring onions, and all the fresh herbs. Toss to combine. Serve scattered with crisp fried shallots.

IGNASI MONREAL
Aioli Munchies

Cooking isn't a highlight of my skill set, but back when I used to live at my mum's place, in my late-teenage stoner years, I would make myself aioli when I got munchies in the middle of the night. Aioli's origins date back to the Roman Empire, which borrowed the recipe from the Egyptians and spread it (pun intended) over the Mediterranean. It is believed that Andalusians then would have introduced it to northern Spain, and for some reason that escapes my Google search. It was Catalans and/or Balearic Islanders that finally named it as we know it today. It is normally served as a dipping sauce with paella or barbecue meals, but I love it with a good loaf of bread. Technically, aioli is just oil and garlic. It comes from the Catalan words '*all i oli*', which literally mean 'garlic and oil', but I prefer my mother's version, which is essentially garlic mayo (a sacrilege to the aioli purists). Weird? Yes. Delicious? Absolutely.

INGREDIENTS
1 egg
1 garlic clove (2 if you want the full experience), peeled
300 ml sunflower oil
100 ml extra virgin olive oil
A splash of vinegar
A pinch of salt

Serves 1

METHOD
Crack the egg into a measuring cup and add the rest of the ingredients. Start blending together slowly (important) with the whisk touching the bottom of the cup. When the emulsion starts to come together, begin to slowly lift and move the whisk up and down until you have the desired consistency. And voilà! Let the dipping begin. Warning: try not to kiss anyone for a few hours after eating this snack.

↙ See inside

In the morning, put the dough into a mortar and pound for a few good minutes with a pestle—ah, sorry, we are in the northern hemisphere, so use a food processor to do the job instead. Observe that all latent euphemisms apply here, pounding, mixing, whatever. You need a slightly sticky, pliable dough. This can take about 20 minutes of moderate processing. Scoop out onto a lightly floured surface and roll into a perfect log. Leave to rest for about another hour or so. Then cut the log into equally sized rounds with a sharp knife. Roll each round into the shape of a man or woman. Put them next to each other and put their arms and legs around one another. The original alkaki is more like an infinity shape than a koeksister, but I think in honour of a good marriage, the alkaki should be more like a flawed braid.

Place your married couple gently into well-heated oil and allow them to agonise and bubble up with shock (without breaking apart). Fry until fused, golden brown to slightly darker shade of tan. Fish them out and place them on absorbent paper. Listen to their whistling of relief. Line still-warm couples in a jar and carefully douse them in your favourite sweet syrup—their reward for surviving the harsh vicissitudes of this life that is like a vat of hot oil. Leave the jar open to allow bad reminiscences to evaporate. Cool completely, then lock the jar and turn upside down until all honey or syrup is absorbed. Add more syrup to adjust to how sweet you want the alkaki. You have a free hand since there is no confirmed recipe for a good marriage. Store in the refrigerator and warm up slowly in the oven on demand.

For the tea, heat a full teapot of water slowly until the surface bubbles languidly, not vigorous boiling. Add all ingredients and turn heat down completely to allow tea to brew, ideally for about an hour. Stir occasionally. Serve with alkaki. Tea left in a glass teapot overnight tastes best the next day.

YEMISI ARIBISALA

Alkaki and the Allegory of a Good Marriage

A Northern-Nigerian bride should ideally have warmed alkakis to hand. A grainy, dense, crumbly, honey-infused pastry that breaks off to reveal hidden silken tracks, alkaki is best served freshly made, or larghetto-warmed in the oven, with a cup of Lipton tea or fura de nunu. Alkaki was originally the preserve of Northern-Nigerian aristocrats, who had it for tea or as a dessert. If you are wondering why a new bride needs alkaki, it is because she is going to be getting more than a few relatives coming round after the wedding. She'll be expected to show up radiant, with days-old henna-decorated hands, swathed in trousseau. There might not be a whisking off to honeyed isolation for two, but there is syrup for sousing the pastry: honey, maple, jaggery, boiled sugar cut through with tamarind or fresh limes. Alkaki would be that meditative snack I would make in the middle of the night. Prepared ahead, then silently rolled, braided, and deep-fried. While making the alkaki, I will fashion some bastardised Scheherazade tale because I find story-making and slow-cooking wonderful amatory partners. The tale begins with the help of...

INGREDIENTS

1 cup of bulgur wheat
1½ cup plain flour
9 tbsp non-homogenised yoghurt
1 tsp ground ginger
1 tsp vanilla pod
A pinch of salt
1 tbsp oil
1¼ cup water
Oil for deep frying
Syrup of your choice

For the accompanying tea
5 green cardamom pods, cracked
A pinch of passion flower tea, lemon balm, or lime blossoms
10 cloves
10 black peppercorns
5 alligator peppers (grains of paradise)
2 star anises
¼ vanilla pod
An inch of fresh ginger, sliced or grated depending on heat preference
Fresh lemongrass, cut to preferred length
Rooibos tea, if available

Serves 4–6

METHOD

Alkaki is an appropriate euphemism for a good marriage. From the first ingredient of crushed wheat and imperfect graininess of personalities, to which you add a few handfuls of plain flour, if you can afford the refinement, to help bind rough grains together. Some fermented milk signifies good tradition. You can decide to add yeast, but why allow hypocrisy so early on into the mix? Non-homogenised goat milk yoghurt is perfect in yeast's place. It is gentle, fragrantly wild, and indigenous. It is a slow hand compared to the loudness of yeast. Mix the three ingredients together by hand. Add in the ground ginger for subtle heat, vanilla for oud, a pinch of salt for integrity, and a tablespoon of oil for divine presence. Mix again thoroughly before adding the emotions of water. Leave the mixed dough together for a few hours, possibly overnight.

JOHN JAVIER
Wonton Broth

You would never have caught me ordering a bowl of wontons, let alone wonton soup, until I moved to Hong Kong and ate at Mak's Noodle. It was this wild, revelatory, almost 'coming of age' experience. I've never enjoyed a bowl of soup so much. After that, every time I was sick, hungover, or heartbroken, wonton soup was the answer. It's so comforting, especially late at night. I've tried to recreate it here (albeit without the specialty mushrooms that are difficult to find here in London). I doubt it's better than what I had at Mak's Noodle, but it's just as good and I'm completely fine with that.

INGREDIENTS
1 bunch yellow chives (spring onions work well too)

For the broth
2 white onions, peeled and sliced
100g ginger, peeled and sliced
8 garlic cloves, peeled and sliced
50g dried shrimp
1 tsp whole black peppercorns
1 tsp whole white peppercorns
4L chicken stock
1 tin anchovies, oil drained and discarded
100g sliced jamón

For the prawn wontons
1kg frozen prawn meat, peeled and deveined
1 tbsp roasted white sesame seed powder
1 tsp dashi powder
1 tsp sesame oil
1 tsp MSG
1 tsp sugar
1 tsp salt
½ egg, whipped
16 wonton wrappers

Serves 4

METHOD
In a large pot on medium heat, sweat the onions, ginger, garlic, and shrimp until translucent. Add the peppercorns and cook for 1 minute. Add the stock and bring to a simmer for 1 hour. Turn off the heat and fully submerge the anchovies and jamón. Infuse for 20 minutes before passing through a fine strainer. Allow the liquid to fall gently, making sure not to press down, then discard the solids. Season to taste. For the wontons, chop the prawn meat until it's the texture of coarse mince. Place in a large metal bowl with the sesame powder, dashi powder, sesame oil, MSG, sugar, salt, and egg. Using your hand, mix vigorously for roughly 5 minutes until the mixture thickens and becomes very sticky. Line your chopping board with wonton sheets and place a teaspoon of prawn mix in the centres. Dip your finger in water and rub it around the edges of the sheets, then bring the corners together and pinch the edges firmly to create a 'money bag'. Bring a large pot of salted water to the boil (about 1 teaspoon of salt per litre). Blanch the prawn wontons for about 1 minute, they'll rise to the surface when they're cooked. Strain the wontons and divide into bowls. In a small pot, bring the broth to a boil then pour into the bowls. Cut the yellow chives into 2cm batons (or slice spring onions 1–2mm thick) and garnish.

SARAH BEN ROMDANE
Lablebi

Lablebi—a Tunisian street-food staple that is halfway between a soup and a stew—is the exact opposite of fancy. It's the kind of dish that generates a certain amount of suspicion at first glance, but is actually so full-flavoured and hearty, you end up wanting to eat it again and again. With this recipe for Lablebi, I want to share with you the taste of late summer nights in Mahdia, my father's family town of origin in coastal Tunisia. It is an invitation to some of the memories I cherish the most. I have been spending all my summers in Mahdia since I was born, but now that it is also where I produce my olive oil, KAÏA, I have been able to connect with this place I now call home in an even more profound way. Nothing hits the spot like a warm Lablebi after a long evening out. In Mahdia, no celebration (be it a club night or a traditional wedding) is complete without a Lablebi. Based on chickpeas and stale bread, it is served in deep and large bowls and integrates a variety of flavours, textures, and temperatures. You can pick and choose the toppings you want, but purists will get everything and eat it spicy.

INGREDIENTS

500g chickpeas, soaked overnight, then drained
1½L cold water
3 tbsp olive oil
1 lemon
1 tsp baking soda
Salt and pepper
4 eggs
1 stale baguette, cut into small pieces
Artisanal harissa
Cumin
Capers
2 jars or tins of tuna fillets
KAÏA olive oil (about 1 tbsp per plate)

Serves 4

METHOD

In a large pot (the chickpeas will swell, so remember to think bigger), pour the chickpeas into the cold water and add the olive oil, the juice and peel of the lemon, and the baking soda. Cover with a cloth and let soak overnight at room temperature. The next day, bring to a boil, then reduce heat to medium-low and simmer, stirring occasionally and replacing any water that evaporates, for about 2 hours until the chickpeas are tender. Season with salt and pepper to taste. Bring another large saucepan of water to a boil over medium-high heat. Once the water starts boiling, turn off the heat. Carefully add eggs into the water one at a time and leave them until you are ready to serve (this is how I cook mollet eggs, but you can use another technique). In an individual large bowl, add a handful of bread at the bottom, then pour a ladle or more of the chickpea water with some chickpeas (as much as you'd like). Add the harissa, cumin, capers, salt, and pepper to taste, then the eggs, tuna, and the fragrant olive oil. Mix well and eat it hot.

PÍA LEÓN
Tuber Toast

This is a significant recipe for me because it uses several tubers from the Peruvian land. Tubers have a special meaning for us. They grow, venturing deep inside the land and safeguarding the plant's best, which later becomes food connecting you to the place you come from. Since everyone has good bread at home and a few roots or veggies that can easily replace the Peruvian tubers, this a perfect recipe for a quick, light dinner. Despite its simplicity, this dish not only bursts with flavour but is also fun to look at with its many colours and shapes. It's a bite at once crispy, creamy, sweet, and salty—like the many layers of everything I've seen in my trips to the Andes. Every crop is a spectacle, and every moment is an experience!

INGREDIENTS
A slice of bread
Butter
20g mature cheese

For the lentil puree
150g cooked lentils (or chickpeas)
1 small garlic clove, peeled
A pinch of cumin
A pinch of paprika
15 ml olive oil
A pinch of salt

For the sautéed oca
100g oca (or carrots), laminated in 0.3mm slices
100 ml olive oil
1 garlic clove, peeled
A pinch of coarse salt

For the honey-cooked ulluco
160g ulluco (or beetroot), laminated in 0.3mm slices
40g honey
10g unsalted butter

For the pickled mashua
200g mashua (or pumpkin), laminated in 0.3mm slices
100 ml apple cider vinegar
20g raw cane sugar
100 ml water

Serves 1

METHOD
To make the lentil puree, blend all the ingredients together until smooth, adding water if needed. Sauté the laminated oca in the oil along with the garlic and salt. For the ulluco, melt the butter and honey over medium heat in a saucepan. Make sure the honey doesn't burn. Add in the laminated ulluco, stirring until it melts. Next mix the vinegar, sugar, and water together in another saucepan and boil for 5 minutes, diluting all ingredients. Let it cool. Place the laminated mashua in a recipient and pour the boiled mixture over it. Cool in the fridge. On the bread, spread butter first and then about 50g of the lentil puree. Cover with around 80g of the ulluco. Heat in the oven at 180ºC for 4 minutes. Place 3 slices of sautéed oca on top, add 5 slices of pickled mashua, and cover everything with cheese.

THE SLEEPING CHEF
ZZZZZZ

JOHN WURDEMAN
Wild Greens and Curded Whey Khinkali

The khinkali is a dumpling believed to originate from the East Georgian highland regions of Khevsureti and Tusheti. Some feel it comes from Central Asia or Mongolia. In language and many aspects of culture, the ebb and flow along the Silk Road was very fluid. Georgia was one of the oldest settled farming communities and had some of the most ancient cities in the region, so what was brought here or taken to a foreign land is difficult to unravel. Georgians celebrate khinkali as a treasured part of their cuisine regardless. The classic version is made of various meats, usually mutton or beef. Also traditional are cheese curds, potatoes, or mushrooms, and in Kist regions, stinging nettles. In Meskheti, a southern mountainous region, they are small, bite-sized, and smothered in caramelised onions and clarified butter. In the city, a blend of pork and beef with lots of herbs is common. It's traditional in both regions to fry leftover khinkali for late-night munchies or a hangover, washed down by a short or two of Chacha. Over the years in my restaurants, we've offered spins on the classic and have been reprimanded by highlanders who thought we'd crossed a sacred line. Here I'd like to offer a creative version that even the conservative locals have embraced, that we continue to serve at Poliphonia Tbilisi, and that is lovely refried late at night!

INGREDIENTS

For the filling

100g soft cottage cheese
100g curded whey
200g stinging nettles (chickweed, beet leaves, or spinach work too) blanched, squeezed, then chopped
50g basil
A pinch of chilli flakes (Aleppo or chipotle recommended)
Salt

For the sauce

100g sour cream
50g coriander leaves
½ garlic clove
Salt and black pepper

For the dough

200g flour
A pinch of salt
Water as needed to make a firm dough

Serves 2–3

METHOD

For the filling and sauce, simply blend the ingredients. The dough is made much like a pasta dough: stir the flour and salt, make a well for the water, stir again, then knead on a lightly floured surface. Roll the dough out to 3–4mm, then using a glass or cup with 7cm diameter, cut out rounds and roll again until they are 14cm in diameter. Place the filling mixture in the centres then close the dumplings, folding the dough edge like an accordion and gathering at the top to form a pouch. Seal by pinching the top firmly and twisting. (Best to watch some videos on YouTube!) Drop the khinkali into gently boiling salty water and stir carefully with a wooden spoon until they float to the top. Take one out and taste to check it's cooked. You can serve fresh with sauce drizzled on the top, or if you're frying them, make sure the dough goes golden and very crispy and put the sauce on the side.

THE CHEF
THE FOOD
...IN THE NIGHT
(A CAT)

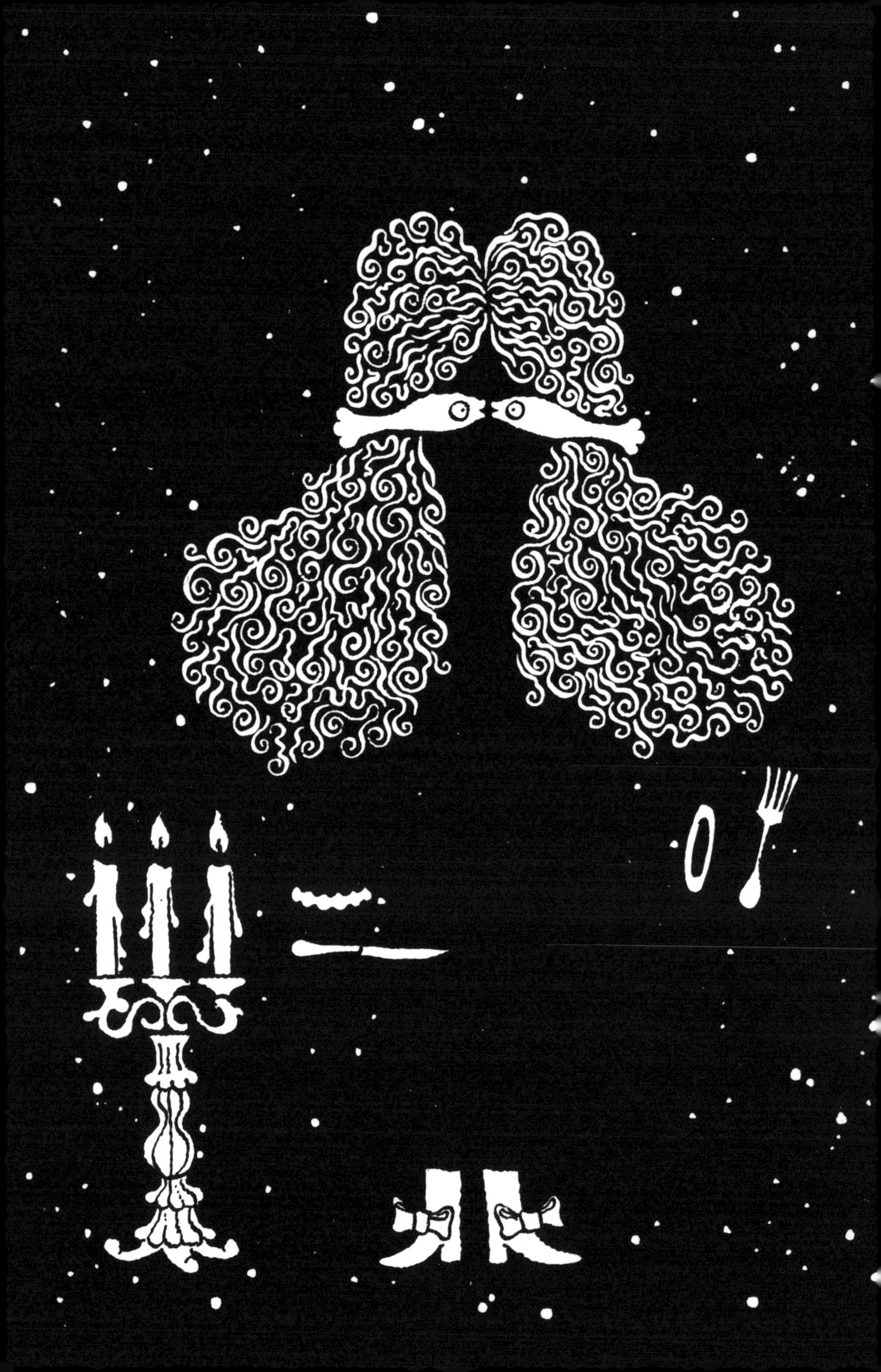

ELLIE BOUHADANA
Spaghetti with Anchovy Butter, Garlic, and Chilli

After a long dinner service and a glass of vermouth with my team, I get home and open the fridge. A snack is needed before a hot shower and bed. My eyes lock on to the whipped anchovy butter that I made earlier in the week. I scan the pantry and there is half a box of thick spaghetti. I am tired and could potentially skip a snack altogether, but I find myself placing a pan on the stove and watching the anchovy butter melt down into a puddle of fragrant oil. Suddenly I am slicing garlic and softening it in the butter. I run my finger through the sauce, it is thick and rich. Lick. I have been a lover of small, salty tinned fish since I was a child, and along with fries or a piece of toast with cheese, it is my ideal snack after cooking for others all day or a night out. The strands of spaghetti become wet and silky from their toss in the pan with the pasta water, a glug of olive oil, a pinch of chilli. The quantities and ingredients are not strict, you can play with them depending on how many people are standing around the kitchen, your love of tinned fish, and what your eyes are drawn to in your fridge. Not so much a recipe, this is more of a template—hot pan, a knob of butter, something salty, and a packet of spaghetti.

INGREDIENTS

440g spaghetti
8 garlic cloves, finely sliced
Extra virgin olive oil
A handful of parsley, finely chopped
Red chilli flakes
Freshly ground black pepper
Flaky salt and fine sea salt

For the whipped anchovy butter
200g good quality butter, cubed and sitting at room temperature
100g best anchovies you can buy, packed in olive oil
1 tsp extra virgin olive oil

Serves 4

METHOD

Place the butter in the bowl of a stand mixer fitted with a whisk and begin whipping for about a minute, until the butter is soft and a little fluffy. Chop the anchovies finely until they resemble a paste. Add them to the bowl along with the olive oil and whisk again for a couple of minutes to evenly incorporate them. Bring a pot of water to a boil, season generously with fine sea salt, stir, then add the spaghetti. While the pasta cooks, place a wide pan on the stove over a medium heat and warm 1 tbsp of the anchovy butter and 1 tbsp of olive oil per person. Once the butter has melted and begins to sizzle gently, add the garlic, a pinch of chilli, and a generous amount of freshly ground black pepper, and nudge everything around the pan. When the garlic smells fragrant and the butter starts to foam, use tongs to pull the pasta out of the water and drop it into the pan. Throw over the parsley, pour in a small ladle of the pasta water, shake the pan, and stir everything energetically until each strand is coated in a silky sauce. If it seems dry, add another splash of pasta water and stir to emulsify. Taste and season with flaky salt. Serve right away on simple plates and eat while hovering over the kitchen bench.

NIKI NAKAZAWA
Salsa de Huevo

Salsa de huevo is one of my all-time favourite comfort dishes. This perfect plate of food was first served to me at the home of one of the mezcal producers I work with in the Sierra Sur of Oaxaca, and since then, I order it whenever available at roadside *comedores* along Highway 175. While this is a very simple dish to prepare, I actually didn't know the secret to making the eggs until recently, after taking a cooking class at the wonderful Thalía Barrios García's Cocina de Humo in Oaxaca City. The technique involves pouring the beaten eggs into a lot of very hot oil in a small (15cm) non-stick pot or sauté pan so that the egg puffs up like a soufflé. Now that I know this trick, I only ever want to eat puffy eggs, whether in salsa, or Thai-style (Khai Jiao), and especially on the late-night shift. In this version of salsa de huevo, I include fish sauce in the egg, because, if you know me, you know that I put fish sauce in everything and it's just one of my favourite seasonings. The salsa can be prepared in a blender or by hand in a *molcajete* (or a pestle and mortar) if you want it to be chunky, just make sure that the tomatoes are fully cooked, or the sauce might taste too raw. I also highly encourage you to accompany it with saucy black beans and tortillas.

INGREDIENTS
2 medium room-temperature eggs
¼ cup plain vegetable oil
1 tsp Thai fish sauce or a pinch of salt

For the salsa
1 onion
4 garlic cloves, unpeeled
2 tomatoes
1 serrano pepper
1 cup chicken stock or water
4 epazote leaves

Serves 2

METHOD
Roast the onion, unpeeled garlic, tomatoes, and whole serrano pepper on a dry skillet or *comal*. Peel the garlic and blend it with the onion, pepper, and tomatoes. Strain the liquid into a pot with a tablespoon of oil and cook with a cup of chicken stock or water and the fresh epazote for about 8–10 minutes. Beat the eggs with the fish sauce or salt until frothy. Heat a small sauté pan, wok, or non-stick pan with half an inch of oil. Make sure the oil is very hot by testing a small amount of egg. If it puffs up immediately, the oil is ready. Pour the egg mixture into the hot oil, wait until the bottom of the 'omelette' browns, and then flip to finish cooking the other side. Remove the egg from the oil and allow to drain onto some paper towels. Place the cooked egg into the salsa and let cook for another couple of minutes. Serve with black beans and eat with hot tortillas or white rice.

FADI KATTAN
Late-Night Labaneh

Imagine, you come home late at night after a long service, you have cooked all day, barely had time to eat anything, and your head is full of recipes, ideas on improvement of things you plated that night, flavours you worked with until they permeate through your palate, and you are hungry! You open your fridge, and go for everything that looks refreshing, comforting. Flavours of your childhood and flavours of zingy freshness, all on a plate as you are eager to sit down, rest your tired legs, and start writing those ideas down before you forget. A plate, a layer of labaneh, maybe the one you prepared a few days ago, maybe one out of a box from your dairy shop, then a finely sliced green onion, a sliced cucumber pickle, slices of fresh cucumber, some roquette, coriander and mint leaves you tear coarsely with your hands, a generous sprinkle of sumac, and those nuts you had toasted earlier for some dish, almonds and pine nuts, and finally a generous dash of olive oil. The first time I assembled this plate, I had just finished serving dinner at Fawda, my Bethlehem restaurant—I still remember the main course that day being slow-cooked lamb neck effiloché. On the walk back home across the deserted alleyways of the Bethlehem souk, my thoughts were all over next day's menu. We had a booking for a private event and I was trying to come up with a menu that reflected the different Palestinian terroirs while celebrating the local ingredients that would be in the market the following day. As soon as I got home, a few ideas popped up and I urgently felt that I needed to write them down. And that is when it happened, my body remembered, I had eaten nothing since breakfast.

INGREDIENTS
80g labaneh
1 spring onion
1 pickled cucumber
1 fresh cucumber
¼ bunch rocket
2 coriander sprigs
2 mint sprigs
1 tsp sumac
1 tsp toasted almonds or pine nuts
2 tsp extra virgin olive oil

Serves 1–2

METHOD
Spread the labaneh in a circle or in a mound in a deep bowl. Slice the spring onion lengthwise, and then cut their length in half. Cut the pickled cucumber and fresh cucumber in half lengthwise then in half again to create bâtonnets. Pop all of those onto the labaneh. With your hands, tear the leaves coarsely and throw them onto the plate. Sprinkle the sumac and nuts on top. Distribute the olive oil evenly to finish.

MASAHIDE IKUTA
Onion Soup with Bone Marrow

A late meal, for me, is soupe à l'oignon. It's a traditional French recipe, perfect to eat late at night when you've drunk too much, or the day after. It's also a winter dish—when you're truly cold, make a soft onion soup au gratin with Comté cheese. The preparation takes time, but it's worth it. Remember to make sure the onions caramelise really well, then you can work on making a white stock with the bone marrow and some very good pepper.

INGREDIENTS
6 onions, peeled and minced
5kg bone marrow
1 bay leaf
Salt and pepper
Baguette, sliced
Comté cheese 24-month matured, grated

Serves 10–12

METHOD
Sweat the onion gently in a saucepan until it caramelises. In another pan, place the bone marrow in water and heat until boiling. Wait until it's well skimmed, then lower the heat, add the bay leaf, a pinch of salt and pepper, and leave for 2 hours. Once cooked, remove all the marrow from the broth, even the bone. Add the caramelised onion and reduce half the broth. Season to taste, place in a soup tureen, and add the sliced baguette and grated cheese on top. Heat the oven to 200ºC and place the tureen inside for 15 minutes, until browned.

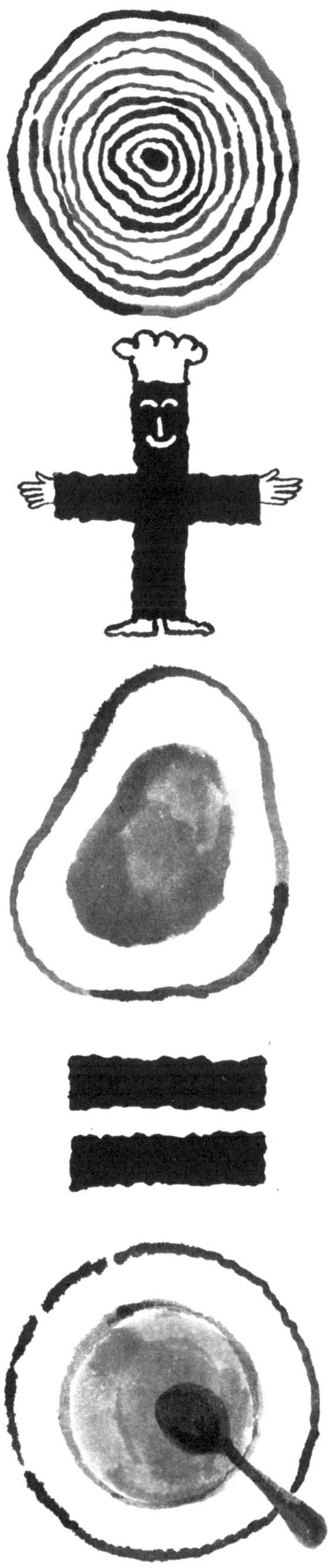

↙ See inside

but to each his own. Crush it using the side of the knife. Then the anchovies, treated as the garlic. This is the one time-hurdle really. That goes in a bowl (a prep bowl, not the salad bowl). Then some but not wild amounts of Worcester sauce. Then several egg yolk (yellow in case you forget) parts only (reasonably fresh and reliable eggs because we are not cooking them). Side note: you can of course do something else with the white part but not late at night I suppose. To separate you crack the egg in half and pass the yolk between shell halves, letting white fall out. I find this charming. Then you mix and pour oil in, slowly. This is called emulsifying. This is to say the egg/garlic/anchovies/oil are becoming one. What is the difference between emulsion, mix, and combine? (Seems like a big word.) Then salt and pepper. Some Dijon mustard. Then lemon juice, as desired, but at least some. Maybe some lemon zest. Parmesan shaved into dressing with a Microplane.

Romaine lettuce. Note about salad spinners: why are all salad spinners so ugly? Also, so much plastic. Big leaves are preferable to little gems because they are grand. You need to clean the salad, unfortunately, though it is a good task to give to someone who is asking to help, assuming that you have someone around at this late hour. Tell them not to rip the leaves, unless you don't care. Anyway, clean and dry the leaves and leave them whole (keep these from wilting and/or getting warm). Come time, which late night is now, just before serving, roll up your sleeves and mix in dressing, such that every leaf is coated.

Add croutons after dressing, on top or mixed in. And, shaved parmesan (yes, parmesan twice). Shaving parmesan requires a new tool choice but that is up to you. Long-winded but the garlic and anchovies are the most time-consuming part of the job, as mentioned.

Or, just make a vinaigrette (certainly easier). Press (nice tool) the garlic cloves. Add Dijon mustard and vinegar, then olive oil, three times the amount of the rest of the ingredients. Meaning it is half oil.

One could add pomegranate seeds. One could add nuts. To roast them, add a little bit of olive oil to a cast-iron pan with medium heat. Stir constantly. Toasting turns to burning seconds after it is brown and perfect, as noted with croutons.

SAM CHERMAYEFF
Caesar Salad with Croutons

It is so great that American culinary ideas are named after people. And this one is actually Mexican. Anyway, it is certainly American now. It is regularly done with all sorts of variations on the classic. This food makes me think of Frank Sinatra. It is a creamy sauce, yes, but the real story is about crunch, i.e. croutons.

INGREDIENTS
1 head Romaine lettuce
Parmesan

For the croutons
1 baguette
Olive oil
Salt and pepper

For the dressing
Garlic, to taste
Worcester sauce (quality matters but L&P works, and it is pronounced 'Woster', please)
Anchovies, to taste (same amount as garlic)
Several eggs
Good olive oil (quality matters because it is a main ingredient)
Salt and pepper
Dijon mustard
1 lemon
More parmesan

For a vinaigrette
3 or more garlic cloves
1 (big fat) tbsp Dijon mustard
White vinegar
Olive oil

Serves 2–4

METHOD
For the croutons (which work on their own really), slice a baguette as thin as possible (no more than 3mm but thinner is better). If older, we suggest a serrated knife. If fresher, then a super sharp knife. It is nice on the bias @ 45°, but maybe not worth the trouble late at night (most of the time it would be good to see through the slices). The effort of this thinness seems and is significant, this makes such a difference. This is a place where time belongs. Place slices in a bowl and toss to cover with olive oil (a lot) and s+p. It is essential to really coat the bread at all points. 'When I say salt I mean Maldon'—Gwyneth Paltrow. (Salt matters, I usually overdo it here slightly.) In theory some thyme or rosemary could be added if desired (but not, we would say, for a Caesar Salad).
Place in oven, not too crowded. This, like toasting of all sorts, has a perfect moment, i.e. the 'done' moment is short. I mean you can burn it. Ovens are different. See times and temps for oven understanding but I would say 190°C for 12 minutes, at least check after 10 (it also works in a pan but the oven allows for more spreading, which is handy). When done, sometimes you need to wait 5 mins before eating, the flavour changes as it cools. Careful not to put hot croutons on chilled salad, which wilts the lettuce and, well...
Back to the salad (dressing). Tons of garlic, diced, then diced more. Then turned into a paste. Somehow the raw garlic overpowers if you press it with a press

CHIARA STROBL
Grießnockerlsuppe

After a long shift at the restaurant, I can't look at any more food. It's the same with my beloved colleagues after spending more than 10 hours in the kitchen together. Many times we've ended up at the bar of the restaurant or a Berliner *Eckkneipe* for a few after-work drinks, talking about the evening service drowned in adrenaline, pride, fun, sweat, and endorphins. With those emotions in my backpack, the drinks in my belly, I cycle home through Kreuzberg at night, and with the wind in my face, my appetite returns in a flash, along with my to-do list. I need to forage herbs for tomorrow! Gleisdreieck Park is a famous destination, you might find chefs from Berlin's fine-dining scene searching between the bushes. I jump off my bike and pull out my torch to look for earthy-tasting ground ivy, nutty, light-green goose weed, and classy mugwort. Arriving home, I dedicate my thoughts to my favourite dish, the thing I'd order as my last supper (if I'd been caught cycling drunk and stealing herbs): Grießnockerlsuppe.

INGREDIENTS
Mix of freshly picked herbs

For the chicken broth
500g onions
300g carrots
1 leek
300g celeriac
1 organic chicken
200g parsley roots
1 bunch parsley
4 juniper berries
2 bay leaves
Salt

For the Grießnockerl
50g butter
1 egg
A pinch of salt
Nutmeg
100g semolina

Serves 4

METHOD
Be lazy and roughly cut the veggies—peeling is overrated. (There's lots of taste and vitamins in the skins, but make sure to wash everything well.) Say thank you to the old chicken that provided us with so many eggs over its lifetime. Look inside, the farmer may have sold you the heart, liver, and lungs, which you could take out and use for another dish. Place the animal in a big pot, cover with water, and slowly bring to a boil. Skim the greyish foam off and simmer. Add the herbs, vegetables, and some salt, and simmer until you can't wait any longer. For the Grießnockerl, take the butter and whisk until creamy. Add the egg, salt, and nutmeg, and whisk again. Stir in the semolina, then give the dough a 15-minute rest. Use that time to wash the herbs from the park—you don't want dog pee on them. Bring a pot of slightly salty water to a boil, and now to form our chic Nockerl dumplings. Get two moist teaspoons and use one to scoop the dough from the other to shape those Austrian triangular beauties. Throw them in the water and gently simmer for 20 minutes until the semolina has soaked up all of the delicious butter. Serve the soup with a few slices of chicken breast, a carrot, the cloud-like dumplings, and don't forget your thieved green topping.

PALINUROBAR
Sandwich with Alacce, Camembert, and Preserved Lemon

Is there a name for that special sort of melancholy that involves the sea, and only the sea? It's a never-ending longing for water, salty breeze, that particular silence which is not in fact silence at all, but the constant murmuring of the waves breaking in the distance, one against the other, forever. And not always hot weather, not always crowded beaches, not always light feelings—it's not (only) about that. Whatever you call this annoying disease, we have it. Some might say it's part of the Italian disposition. This is maybe why we decided to open a place called Palinurobar, and to name it after an obscure Italian song from the '80s that portrays a summer day spent in a bar on the beach in Palinuro, not so far from Napoli. Maybe it's not the main reason, but surely one of the most prominent. We long for the sea because we don't live close to it, so what do you do when you live in a city like Milano, an hour and 30 minutes from the closest drop of seawater? You dream of it. Sometimes, though, you might need a little booster to those dreams. You might need something to eat. The melancholy usually gets you at night. Light already faded, you're back home but not ready for bed, not yet. You look out the window just to see other windows. There's too much artificial light for the stars to be seen. No waves in the distance, just the frenzied echo of the last cars. That's the moment. Reach for the larder. Make yourself a sandwich. A little Mediterranean fantasy.

INGREDIENTS

Alacce sott'olio
Buffalo camembert
Focaccia or preferred bread
Preserved lemons
Thyme
Pepper

Serves 1

METHOD

Alacce are a sort of anchovies, just bigger and fatter. Thus, better for a late-night snack. They aren't easy to find, and that's another good thing: the quality is usually high, whatever kind of alacce you get your hands on. They should come in fillets preserved in olive oil. Take a few of them, let them drain, and put them aside. Camembert is a French cheese that works perfectly fine with this kind of fish. Who said that seafood and cheese shouldn't go hand in hand? It's not originally from the Mediterranean area but from Normandy, northern France. We chose the one made with bufala (buffalo) milk, usually made in Campania, South Italy, for a lighter taste and another glimpse of the seaside. Cut a few pieces of cheese, put them into the bread. As for the bread, every good bread works fine (not multi-seed though, and not rye bread), but pizza-like bread is perfect when cut in half. Heat the bread and the cheese under a hot plate until the camembert begins to melt. Preserved lemons are a Moroccan specialty, and are kept in their juice and a lot of salt. They last months, and in the process they become mellow, not so acidic, and of course savoury. Discard the pulp, use only a quarter of the skin. Cut it thinly and rinse it under cool water a bit. Put the alacce and the lemon in the sandwich. Season with thyme and pepper.

JON GRAY
Chocolate Waffles with Berries and Spicy Maple

I like to keep things simple, which is why we created a waffle and pancake mix that's 'just add water'. Our blends use ancestral ingredients like cassava root for antioxidants and trace minerals, and sorghum flour, an ancestral grain originally cultivated over 10,000 years ago in the East African regions now known as Sudan and Ethiopia. Sorghum has been documented as a food and fibre source as far back as 7th century BC Egyptian wall art and archaeology. The chocolate aka the Black Power waffle really hits when I'm craving a decadent treat or am trying to finesse a dessert without having to mise out ingredients. I may be called the dishwasher but that doesn't mean I'm trying to spend the night cleaning up. The topping here calls for seasonal berries along with pure maple syrup and your choice of chilli flakes. Flaky salt enhances the flavours of the chocolate, berries, and syrup for an unforgettable combo that's easy on the eyes as it lingers on the palate. It's only four ingredients so the quality of each one should be top of mind. The blacker the berry, the sweeter the juice. Don't slip on that drip, ya heard?

INGREDIENTS
120g Ghetto Gastro Chocolate WAVY Waffle Mix
100g water

For the topping
1 cup fresh berries (whatever is freshest at the market, you eat with your eyes first)
¼ cup maple syrup
½ tsp smoked chipotle flakes or other dried chilli of your choice
A pinch of flaky salt

Serves 2

METHOD
Heat waffle iron to medium-high—we like our waffles crisp. In a small mixing bowl, combine the waffle mix and water and stir until smooth. Pour an even layer onto the waffle iron, then close and turn it on. Cook for about 5 minutes, or until the waffle is crisp on the outside and cooked on the inside (as always, follow the instructions for your particular waffle maker). While the waffle cooks, toss together the berries, maple syrup, chilli flakes, and salt. The berries will macerate with the syrup, chillies, and salt to create a spicy, berry-infused topping. Cut the finished waffle into quarters and divide onto two plates. Spoon the berries over top, then tip the bowl and drizzle the infused maple syrup over the waffle and the berries.

Apartamento Cookbook #7: Late-Night Meals

First edition: December 2022
Published by Apartamento Publishing S.L.

Concept and Art Direction:
Apartamento Studios

Drawings: Benoît François
Editorial Director: Robbie Whitehead
Managing Editor: Madeleine Willis

Bruc 49 3-2
08009 Barcelona
Spain
info@apartamentomagazine.com
www.apartamentomagazine.com

ISBN: 978-84-09-46100-4

Printed in Barcelona

The publisher will donate 20% of the profits generated by this book to The Enriqueta Villavecchia Private Foundation for Child Oncology.

The Enriqueta Villavecchia Private Foundation for Child Oncology, established in Barcelona in 1989, is a nonprofit organisation with charitable and welfare aims to provide integral care for children and young people undergoing oncological treatment in Catalonia and to provide support to their families.